T0129463

Isaiah 26:3-4
"PERFECT PEACE"

Isaiah 26:3-4
"Perfect Peace XVI"

Shoes

Vanessa Rayner

authorHOUSE®

AuthorHouse™
1663 Liberty Drive
Bloomington, IN 47403
www.authorhouse.com
Phone: 1 (800) 839-8640

Published by AuthorHouse

ISBN: 978-1-5462-6656-3 (sc)
ISBN: 978-1-5462-6657-0 (e)

Library of Congress Control Number: 2018913088

Print information available on the last page.

Contents

A Gift . . .

A walk with the Lord . . .
Begins with a single step with or without shoes.

Theme

The message of **Isaiah 26:3-4** is "Perfect Peace." This is the distinct and unifying composition of this book with the subtitle **Shoes**.

<u>A Song of Praise</u>

You will keep in perfect peace those
whose minds are steadfast,
Trust in the Lord forever, for the Lord, the
Lord himself, is the Rock eternal.
Isaiah 26:3-4 NIV

Prayer

Oh, Heavenly Father,
I thank you for another day. I thank you
for another day. Glory be to God!
Father, you been good to me. Hallelujah!
I pray that your people and their
families are being blessed, also.

Oh, Heavenly Father,
I ask in Jesus' name that the Holy Spirit will
help readers to remember Your word.
I pray the word of God will give them
peace when they need it the most.
Thank you, Father, for blessing those
that help Your work go forth.

Oh, Heavenly Father,
Your word made it clear that You will
reward those that bless your servant.
It could be through prayer, words of
encouragement, to giving that person
a cup of water.

Mark 9:41 states,
If anyone gives you even a cup of water
because you belong to the Messiah,

I tell you the truth, that person will
surely be rewarded; NLT.

Oh, Heavenly Father,
I give you all the Glory, Honor and Praise in Jesus' name.

Amen.

Author's Notes

Author notes generally provide a way to add extra information to one's book that may be awkward and inappropriate to include in the text of the book itself. It offers supplemental contextual details on the aspects of the book. It can help readers understand the book content and the background details of the book better. The times and dates of researching, reading, and gathering this information are not included; mostly when I typed on it.

1640; Wednesday, 11 July 2018; I started working on this book. On July 9, 2018, I finished proofreading book XV. Since then I have been praying and asking Father God what's next. I woke up this morning with "shoes" on my mind, and it stayed on my mind throughout my workday. I'm not a shoe-person and haven't brought a pair this year; for real. But as I was unlocking my front door to enter my home, it came to my mind to count my shoes. ?, yes, ???, I thought, what harm in it, so, I did.

I counted:

1 pair of Rider Shower Sandals

1 pair of Bowling Shoes

1 pair of Flip Flops

1 pair of Naturalizer N5 Peek Toe Heels

1 pair of Under Armour Running Shoes

1 pairs of Rocky Work Boots

1 pairs of H2K Slides

1 pairs of Laura Ashley slip on house shoes

2 pairs of Air-Walker Mules

2 pairs of Leisure Boots

2 pairs of work shoes by Timberland Pro and Rocky

2 pairs of tennis shoes by Champion and Fila.

3 pairs of open toe sandals by American Eagle, Glo Jean, and Montego Bay Club

4 pairs of wedge heel shoes by Thom McAn (2), Clark Collection, and Classic Elem

When I finished, Father said, "write about shoes." I assumed in the Bible.

1623; Thursday, 12 July 2018

1650; Friday, 13 July 2018

0848; Saturday, 14 July 2018

1617; Thursday, 19 July 2018; Happy Birthday Mom, "Ulyer Moore" RIP

0412; Saturday, 21 July 2018

0736; Sunday, 22 July 2018

2103; Monday, 23 July 2018

1639; Thursday, 26 July 2018; Happy Birthday Sister, "Regina C. Moore."

2103; Friday, 27 July 2018

2059; Saturday, 28 July 2018; I attended Apostle Cary Lee Allen's sister funeral, Ivy Crudup in Forest, MS at noon. Then attended his Prayer Line this evening at 7 pm. God is good, all the time.

0838; Sunday, 29 July 2018

2256; Monday, 30 July 2018

0000; Tuesday, 31 July 2018

0000; Wednesday, 01 August 2018

0000; Thursday, 02 August 2018

0706; Sunday, 05 August 2018; I started a water-fast on Friday, 08/03/18 at 1430. I worked on Father's book 8 days straight, and I'm still wrestling with the 1st chapter. I'm struggling to make it read and feel comforting in my innermost being. I'm planning on ending this fast on

08/08/18 at 0800, in Jesus' Name. The number 8 signifies "Resurrection and Regeneration." Praise God!

1956; Thursday, 09 August 2018

1728; Friday, 10 August 2018

0217; Saturday, 11 August 2018

1827; Sunday, 12 August 2018

1622; Monday, 13 August 2018

1635; Tuesday, 14 August 2018

1201; Wednesday, 15 August 2018

2010; Thursday, 16 August 2018

1718; Wednesday, 22 August 2018

1635; Thursday, 23 August 2018

1705; Tuesday, 28 August 2018

1732; Thursday, 30 August 2018

1631; Friday, 31 August 2018

0608; Saturday, 01 September 2018

0000; Sunday, 02 September 2018

0000; Monday, 03 September 2018

1715; Tuesday, 04 September 2018

1631; Wednesday, 05 September 2018

1749; Thursday, 06 September 2018; RIP Happy B'day Father ~ Rev. Ambous Moore

2155; Friday, 07 September 2018

0735; Saturday, 08 September 2018

0910; Sunday, 09 September 2018

1635; Tuesday, 11 September 2018

1647; Wednesday, 12 September 2018

1635; Thursday, 13 September 2018; Happy B'day ~ Lil Charles Jr.

0107; Saturday, 15 September 2018; Just left Minister Myrtle's Midnight Prayer Line. Praise God!

0900; Sunday, 16 September 2018

1831; Monday, 17 September 2018

1622; Tuesday, 18 September 2018

1732; Thursday, 20 September 2018

1727; Friday, 21 September 2018; Hand/Wrist/Forearm pain day; came home very early from work, just woke up not too long ago. Hallelujah! My mind is still on the Almighty.

0534; Saturday, 22 September 2018

0555; Sunday, 23 September 2018

0637; Monday, 24 September 2018

0548; Tuesday, 25 September 2018; Crazy painful morning. I'm going to read/type until I can't keep my eyes open. Praise God.

1726; Wednesday, 26 September 2018

1744; Thursday, 27 September 2018

1261; Sunday, 30 September 2018

1706; Monday, 01 October 2018

1639; Wednesday, 03 October 2018

1640; Thursday, 04 October 2018

1714; Friday, 05 October 2018

1646; Tuesday, 09 October 2018

1629; Wednesday, 10 October 2018

1703; Thursday, 11 October 2018

1735; Friday, 12 October 2018

0526; Saturday, 13 October 2018

0825; Sunday, 14 October 2018

1629; Tuesday, 16 October 2018; I'm basically finished; a little more proofreading will do.

0436; Sunday, 21 October 2018

1735; Tuesday, 23 October 2018

1651; Thursday, 25 October 2018

1623; Friday, 26 October 2018; Preparing to send book materials to AuthorHouse.

Preface

Isaiah 26:3-4, "Perfect Peace XVI"
Shoes

The book <u>Isaiah 26:3-4, "Perfect Peace XVI" Shoes</u> is the 16th book in a series called Isaiah 26:3-4, "Perfect Peace." Praise God!

It all started from how I drew near to the LORD in my workplace by keeping my mind on Him. I related numbers you see throughout the day, everywhere, on almost everything on Him, His word, biblical events, and facts to give me peace in the midst of chaos.

It's our desire for you to discover the power of the Holy Spirit by numbers, words, places, people, and things related to the word "shoes."

Remember, the LORD Jesus <u>PROMISED us tribulation</u> while we were in this world.

These things, I have spoken unto you,
that in me ye might have peace.
In the world ye shall have tribulation:
But be of good cheer; I have overcome the world.
John 16:33 KJV

However, we have been <u>PROMISED His peace</u> while we endure these trials, tribulations, troubles, and tests. Perfect

Peace is given only to those whose mind and heart reclines upon the LORD. God's peace is increased in us according to the knowledge of His Holy Word.

> **Grace and peace be multiplied unto you**
> **through the knowledge of God,**
> **and of Jesus our LORD.**
> *2* Peter 1:2 KJV

Thanks... To the Readers of the world

As a disciple of the LORD Jesus Christ, I have learned true success comes when we are seeking and striving to do God's purpose for our lives. Our real happiness lies in doing God's will; not in fame and fortune.

I appreciate your support. Thanks for helping me spread "Perfect Peace" through your e-mail, Facebook, Twitter, LinkedIn, Instagram, Tumblr, Messenger and or other accounts to your family, friends, neighbors, co-workers, church family, internet social friends, and associates.

Remember, you may not know until you get to heaven just how much a song you sung, kind words spoken by you or even a book you suggested reading, at the right moment, encourage a person to keep on going when a few minutes before they were tempted to give up on life and their walk with the LORD.

Your lovingkindness to this ministry is greatly appreciate.

Note of Interests: Lovingkindness is a unique kind of love. It's the English translation for the Hebrew word "chesed." This form of love is characterized by acts of kindness, motivated by love. The word "lovingkindness" is used mostly by religious traditions. It is mentioned 29 times in the King James Bible; 23 times in Psalms, 4 times in Jeremiah, once in Isaiah and Hosea. The word "lovingkindness" doesn't occur in the New Testament, but words like brotherly love, goodness, kindness, and mercy correspond to "lovingkindness."

~~~~~~~~~~~~~

Acknowledgements

I wish to express my sincere gratitude to *"Our Heavenly Father"* for his guidance, patience, and lovingkindness throughout the writing of this book.

Introduction

For Those Who Want to Be Kept In "Perfect Peace"

This book was prepared and written to open your mind to a "Perfect Peace" that comes only from God. I'm striving to elevate you into a "Unique and Profound" awareness of God's presence around you at all time.

According to some people, it's hard to keep your mind on the LORD. While most Christians will agree that if you keep your mind stayed on the LORD, He will keep you in "Perfect Peace." This is why so many people enjoy going to church on Sundays and attending midweek services for peace and joy that they receive, but only for a short time.

You can experience the peace of the LORD throughout the day and every day. His unspeakable joy, his strength, his "Perfect Peace" in the midst of the storm whether it's at work, home, college, school, etc. You can also experience this peace, even when your day is going well.

This concept of this book was placed in my spirit by our Father, which art in heaven, to help me when he allowed Satan to test me at my workplace until he finished molding me into a MAP; (Minister/Ambassador/Pastor).

Throughout these pages, I will be focussing on biblical events, and facts surrounding the word "shoes." However, I am sure much more can be said concerning the word "shoes" in the Bible, so these subjects serve merely as an introduction and are not exhaustive by any means.

Dedication

This book is dedicated to the makers of . . .
Rider Shower Sandals
Bowling Shoes
Flip Flops
Naturalizer N5 Peek Toe Heels
Under Armour Running Shoes
Rocky Work Boots
H2K Slides
Laura Ashley (Slip on House Shoes)
Air-Walker Mules
Leisure Boots
Timberland Pro and Rocky (Work Shoes)
Champion and Fila (Tennis Shoes)
American Eagle, Glo Jean, and Montego Bay Club (Sandals)
Thom McAnn, Clark Collection, and Classic Elem (Wedge
Heel Shoes)

Chapter 1

SHOES

The Wikipedia Encyclopedia states that a "shoe" is an item of footwear intended to protect and comfort the human foot. The word "footwear" refers to a garment worn on the feet to protect against the environmental elements.

Shoe styles have changed down through the centuries by cultures and traditions. The earliest known shoes were known as sandals. The bible sandals were flat with no heels and consist of a thin sole with a strap or two. Shoes of that era were made from leather, wood or canvas.

Today, shoes are much more different and have many more purposes. They are made from materials like rubber, plastic, and other durable substance. Some shoes have heels, and others have very high heels. Shoes with high heels are called fashion shoes, while other shoes are called casual shoes. The shoes with no heels are typically called flats, and these are labeled as comfortable casual shoes. Many shoes are designed for specific purposes like boots, hiking boots, skiing boots, tennis shoes, slippers, shower shoes, bowling shoes, running shoes, walking shoes, and safety shoes.

The word "shoes" is mentioned 21 times in the King James Bible; 12 times in the Old Testament, and 9 times in the New Testament. The word "shoe" without the "s" is mentioned 9 times, and only in the Old Testament; Deuteronomy 25:9, Deuteronomy 25:10, Deuteronomy 29:5, Joshua 5:15, Ruth 4:7, Ruth 4:8, Psalm 60:8, Psalm 108:9, and Isaiah 20:2.

***Please take a moment and read each biblical event that surrounds each one; you will be enlightened. Psalm 60:8 and Psalm 108:9 (KJV) wordings are identical.

Note of Interests: The word "shoes" and "sandals" are interchangeable in "The Word of God." The word "shoes" is not mentioned in the NIV but "sandals;" and it's mentioned 28 times. In the NLT, "sandals" is mentioned 25 times, and the word "shoes" is mentioned once in Ephesians 6.

> **"For shoes, put on the peace that**
> **comes from the Good News**
> **so that you will be fully prepared."**
> Ephesians 6:15 NLT

~~~~~~~~~~~

The King James Bible (KJB) is also called King James Version (KJV) and the Authorized Version (AV). It's an English translation of the Christian Bible authorized by King James I of England. A team of 54 translators begun the translation in 1604, and it was completed in 1611.

The books and chapters in the King James Bible which the word "shoes" is mentioned are listed below.

Old Testament

1. Exodus 3:5
2. Exodus 12:11
3. Deuteronomy 33:25
4. Joshua 9:5
5. Joshua 9:13
6. 1 Kings 2:5
7. Song of Solomon 7:1
8. Isaiah 5:27
9. Ezekiel 24:17
10. Ezekiel 24:23
11. Amos 2:6
12. Amos 8:6

New Testament

1. Matthew 3:11
2. Matthew 10:10
3. Mark 1:7
4. Luke 3:16
5. Luke 10:4
6. Luke 15:22
7. Luke 22:35
8. Acts 7:33
9. Acts 13:25

Note of Interests: The word "sandals" is actually mentioned twice in the King James Bible; Mark 6:9 and Acts 12:8. Mark 6:9 reads, "But be shod with sandals; and not put on two coats," and Acts 12:8 reads, "And the angel said unto him, Gird thyself, and bind on they sandals. And so he did. And he saith unto him, Cast thy garment about thee, and follow me."

~~~~~~~~~~~~

Just for clarity, Acts 12:8 is embedded in Peter's miraculous escape from prison, Acts 12:1 – 18. The angel tells Peter to get dressed and put on his sandals, and then led him out of jail. Mark 6:7 – 12 described when Jesus sent out the 12 disciples. Mark 6:9 was part of Jesus' instructions to the disciples for their journey; the disciples could wear sandals, but no extra shirt. Matthew 10:10 is speaking on the same biblical event as Mark 6:9. However, in Matthew 10:10 the word "shoes" is used instead of "sandals" in the KJV.

Chapter 2

BIBLICAL SANDALS

There are no surviving artifacts of the shoes that Adam and Eve might have worn after they were banished from the Garden of Eden. According to the Scriptures, God made them "coats of skins" to wear, Genesis 3:21. It's believed that the first pair of footwear was made of animal skins since that's what the Lord God clothed Adam and Eve with around 4004 BCE; that's a little over 6000 years ago.

Adam and Eve were created in the image of God, Genesis 1:27. God named the man "Adam" which come from the Hebrew word "adomah" meaning "man" and it signifies "red earth." Adam named the woman who was created from his rib "Eve" which means "life."

Adam and Eve are the first humans created by God, according to Jewish, Islamic, and Christian Religions. It's believed that all humans have descended from them. God created them to take care of His creation, to populate the earth, and to have a relationship with Him.

Note of Interests: According to Jewish tradition, Adam and Eve had 56 children, and Adam lived to be 930 years old.

~~~~~~~~~~~

According to Genesis 2:15, the Lord God placed Adam in the Garden of Eden to work it and keep it. The Lord commanded the man, saying, "You may surely eat of every tree of the garden, but of the "tree of the knowledge of good and evil" you shall not eat, for in the day that you eat of it you shall surely die," Genesis 2:16 – 17.

Note of Interests: When the Lord God forbade Adam from eating the fruit from the "tree of the knowledge of good and evil" Eve wasn't created yet.

~~~~~~~~~~~

Genesis 2:18, God decided it wasn't good for man to be alone. In verses 21 – 23, the Lord made Adam a helper comparable to him, whom Adam called "Woman" and named her "Eve."

In Genesis 3, Eve was deceived by the serpent in the Garden of Eden. He convinced her to eat the fruit from the "tree of the knowledge of good and evil." After she ate, she took the fruit to Adam, and he ate it, knowing he was doing the wrong thing.

In the cool of the day, Adam and Eve heard the voice of the Lord God walking in the garden, and they hid from God presence among the trees, Genesis 3:8. The Lord called unto

Adam, "Where art thou?" and Adam stated he was afraid because he was naked.

Question: How did Adam and Eve try to hide their nakedness?

Answer in the back of the book

The Lord asked Adam who told him that he was naked? Hast thou ate of the tree, of which I commanded thee that thou shouldest not eat? Adam then blames the woman that God gave him for eating from the tree.

When Adam and Eve disobeyed God, they experienced spiritual death from Him. Adam and Eve no longer had a beautiful, carefree life. Man would have to deal with thorns and weeds that would make growing food hard, and the woman would forever give childbirth in pain.

According to Genesis 3:21, God made "coats of skins" for Adam and Eve to wear and banished them from the Garden of Eden. Therefore, scholars believed that the first pair of footwear worn by Adam and Eve were made of animal skins.

The complete biblical event of Adam and Eve can be found in Genesis 1:26 – Genesis 5:5.

Chapter 3

PUT OFF THY SHOES

Exodus 3:5 & Acts 7:33

The first place the word "shoes" is actually mentioned in the Bible is in the Book of Exodus, chapter 3.

And he said, Draw not nigh hither: **put off thy shoes** from off thy feet, for the place whereon thou standest is holy ground. Exodus 3:5 KJV

"Do not come any closer," God said. "Take off your sandals, for the place where you are standing is holy ground." Exodus 3:5 NIV

"Do not come any closer," the Lord warned. "Take off your sandals, for you are standing on holy ground." Exodus 3:5 NLT

Then said the Lord to him, **Put off thy shoes** from thy feet: for the place where thou standest is holy ground. Acts 7:33 KJV

~~~

The King James Version (KJV), New International Version (NIV) and New Living Translation (NLT) of the Bible demonstrate how shoes and sandals are interchangeable, but the concept of the verse is the same.

Note of Interests: The KJV is called a "word-for-word translation." In this Bible translation, the words are mostly matching between languages. The NIV is considered a "thought-for-thought translation." When a Bible is translated "thought-for-thought," it means that the translator(s) has taken the original words and applied an understanding of thought behind the words which is conveyed in the rendering of the verse. NLT is a "paraphrase translation." It attempts to convey some key concepts and basic truths into a language which the typical reader can understand.

~~~~~~~~~~~~

According to Exodus 3:15, Moses is told by God to remove his shoes/sandals from his feet because he is standing on holy ground. Around 14 BC, the Biblical sandals were merely a flat sole, made of wood or palm tree bark, attached to the feet by leather straps called thongs.

Note of Interests: In Joshua 5:15, Joshua is instructed by God to remove his shoe (shoe without the "s" in the KJV; and sandals with an "s" in the NLT; but the concept is the same). The verses read, "And the captain of the Lord's host said unto Joshua, Loose thy shoe from off thy foot; for the place whereon thou standest is holy. And Joshua did so," KJV. The commander of the Lord's army replied, "Take off your sandals, for the place where you are standing is holy. And Joshua did as he was told," NLT.

~~~~~~~~~~~~

Now, let's learn what led up to the Lord telling Moses to, "put off thy shoes." Moses was born in Egypt in the Land of Goshen to Amram and Jochebed. Jochebed was the daughter of Levi, Numbers 26:59. Amram was the son of Kohath, and the grandson of Levi, Exodus 6:18.

Note of Interests: Jochebed married her nephew, Amram. She, therefore, became the wife of Amram, as well as his aunt. Amram was married to his father's sister. Amram and Jochebed were also the parents of Aaron and Miriam, who grew up to be a great prophetess of the Jewish people.

~~~~~~~~~~~~

Amram and Jochebed's younger son, Moses was born around 1400 BC. At this time, the Israelites were enslaved by Egypt, but the increasing numbers of Israelites worried the Egyptian Pharaoh. He feared that the Israelites might become an ally with his enemies. Therefore, Pharaoh ordered that all newborn Hebrew boys to be killed to reduce the population of the Israelites. Moses' parents secretly hid him for 3 months, while Pharaoh had all the newborn babies murdered, Exodus 2.

When Moses' mother realized she could no longer hide him, she made a basket from papyrus reeds. Jochebed places baby Moses in the basket while his sister, Miriam stood at a distance, watching to see what would happen to him.

Note of Interests: Scholars believe that Miriam, Moses' sister was 15 years old at this time, and his brother, Aaron was 3 years old.

~~~~~~~~~~~~

Pharaoh's daughter, the Princess came out to bathe in the Nile River, and her maidens found the child in the river. Moses' sister asked Pharaoh's daughter, "should she find a Hebrew woman to nurse the baby for her," and she, "said yes." Moses' mother is the one who nursed Moses for the Princess. The Princess named the baby Moses, "because she drew him out of the water;" that's what Moses name means. Moses was raised as her own, and he grew up with the Egyptian royal family.

Note of Interests: The Midrash identifies Pharaoh's daughter, the Egyptian Princess as Queen Bithiah; in Hebrew Bitya. In Jewish tradition, she was exiled by the Pharaoh for claiming Moses the Levite as her child. She was the only Egyptian not affected by the plagues, and the only female to survive the 10th and final plague; the death of all firstborns of Egypt. Queen Bithiah left Egypt with Moses during the exodus of the children of Israel, and later married Mered the Judahite from the tribe of Judah, 1 Chronicles 4:17 – 18.

~~~~~~~~~~~~

When Moses became a young adult, he went out among the Hebrews, his people, to observe their hard labor. While he was there, he saw an Egyptian beating one of the Hebrews. Out of anger, Moses killed the Egyptian and hid the body in the sand. When Moses when out the next day, he observed 2 Hebrew men fighting. So, he asked, "why were they attacking fellow Hebrews?" The men asked Moses, "who made him a ruler and judge over them." They also asked Moses, "was he planning on killing them like he killed the Egyptian?"

When Pharaoh heard about this incident, he sought to kill Moses. So, Moses fled and settled by a well in the land of Midian. A priest of Midian had 7 daughters, and they came to water their father's flock at the well. While they were there, some other shepherds tried to drive them away. Moses defended them and watered their flock.

When they returned home early, their father asked, "why are they back so soon, today." They said, "an Egyptian rescued them from the shepherds, drew water for them, and watered the flock!" They thought Moses was an Egyptian.

Their father told them to go and invite the man to come and eat with them. Moses accepted the invitation, and he settled there with them. In time, Reuel gave his daughter named Zipporah to Moses to marriage. They had two sons named Gershom, and Eliezer.

In the meantime, the Israelites continued to groan under their heavy burden of slavery in Egypt. They cried out for help, and their desperate cry went up to God, and God heard their groaning, Exodus 2:24 – 25.

According to Exodus 3, Moses was shepherding the flock of his father-in-law. When he led the flock to the far side of the desert, he came to the mountain of God; Horeb, Exodus 3:1.

The angel of the Lord appeared to Moses in a flame of fire from within a bush. Moses looked up, and the bush was ablaze with fire, but it was not being consumed. Moses thought, he will turn aside to see this amazing sight. When the Lord saw that Moses had turned aside to look, God called to him from within the bush and said, "Moses, Moses!" And Moses said, "Here I am." God said, "Do not approach any closer!" Take your sandals off your feet, for the place where you are standing is holy ground."

The Lord told Moses he had seen the affliction of his people in Egypt and heard their cry. He has come down to deliver them from the hand of the Egyptians and to bring them to a land flowing with milk and honey. He was sending him to Pharaoh to bring His people out of Egypt, Exodus 3:10. Moses said to God, "Who am I, that I should go to Pharaoh, or that I should bring the Israelites out of Egypt?"

The complete life and life accomplishments of Moses, up to his death is recorded in Exodus 1:8 through Deuteronomy 34:8.

The people of Israel mourned for Moses on the plains of Moab for 30 days,

until the customary period of mourning was over.
Deuteronomy 34:8 NLT

The phrase "take off your sandals" is also mentioned in Acts 7, and it's regarding Moses. Beginning at Acts 7, Stephen addressed the Sanhedrin. He explained how God appeared to our ancestor Abraham in Mesopotamia. God told Abraham to leave his native land, his relatives, and go to a land He would show him. So, Abraham left the land of Chaldeans.

Note of Interests: Mesopotamia was the region which is now called Iraq; the land between the Tigris and Euphrates Rivers. Mesopotamia was one of the earliest areas to be inhabited after the Great Flood.

~~~~~~~~~~~~

Beginning at verse 20, Stephen starts telling the crowd the history and events surrounding Moses. Acts 7:33, Stephen stated that the Lord said to Moses, "take off your sandals, for you are standing on holy ground."

Then said the Lord to him,
Put off thy shoes for thy feet:
for the place where thou standest is holy ground.
Acts 7:33 KJV

Stephen goes on to tell the crowd that they are stubborn, heathen at heart, and deaf to the truth. The Jewish Leaders were enraged by Stephen's speech. They dragged him outside the city and stoned him to death, Acts 7:58. As Stephen was being stoned, he fell to his knees and prayed. He asked, "the Lord Jesus to receive his spirit, and don't charge the people with this sin," and he died, Acts 7:60.

Chapter 4

SHOES ON YOUR FEET

Exodus 12:11

And thus, shall ye eat it; with your loins girded, your **shoes on your feet**, and your staff in your hand; and ye shall eat it in haste: it is the Lord's Passover. KJV

~~~

The final plague that God sent against Egypt is recorded in Exodus 12. This plague is different from the others. This plague requires preparation by the Israelites.

Beginning in Exodus 3, God sent Moses to Egypt to deliver and bring His people out of Egypt; the Israelites. The Egyptian Pharaoh did not heed Moses appeal to set the people of Israel free from slavery, at first. God sent 10 plagues upon the Egyptians before they decided to set the Israelites free.

Let's name the 10 plagues that were sent against the Egyptians.

1. _____
2. _____

3. _____
4. _____
5. _____
6. _____
7. _____
8. _____
9. _____
10. _____

Answer is in the back of the book

The 10th plague that God descend upon the people of Egypt was the death of the firstborns in the land. Only those families that sacrificed an unblemished lamb and smeared its blood on the doorposts of the house would be "passed over" from the impending wrath from heaven.

According to Exodus 12:29 – 32, at midnight, the Lord smote the 1st born of every Egyptian family, including Pharaoh only son. The Egyptians were so devastated that Pharaoh calls Moses and Aaron to him during the night and commands them to leave Egypt.

According to Exodus 12:33 – 38, the other Egyptians feared for their life, and they eagerly turn over gold, silver, and clothing to the Israelites, so that they could leave Egypt. The Israelites left the land of Goshen where they had lived for generations. They started their journey toward the southeast, to a city named Succoth. There were approximately 600,000 fighting men, not counting the young boys, women, children and the mixed multitude that left Egypt, Exodus 12:37. Many scholars believe the total number of people was 2.5 million. The Israelites had lived in Egypt for 430 years, but

God brought them out of Egypt, just as He had promised, Exodus 12:40 – 42.

The Passover is the Jewish celebration of God's freeing the Israelites from Egyptian slavery around 1513 BC. God commanded the Israelites to remember that significant event each year on the 14th day of the Jewish month Abib, which was later called Nisan.

The Passover is a one-day holiday that commemorates the Israelites deliverance by the blood of the lamb. The Passover is followed by the Feast of Unleavened Bread that last for the next 7 days.

The 12th chapter of Exodus gives instructions to the Israelites on how to memorialize the events surrounding their salvation from the final plague. The Passover and the Festival of Unleavened Bread were 2 new ordinances commanded by God to the Israelites.

In verses 1 – 11, God tells Moses and Aaron how the nation of Israel is to commemorate the Passover. The instructions are given below:

1. On the 10th day of the 1st Jewish month, Nisan, each man must choose a year-old male lamb or goat, without a blemish for a sacrifice, for his family, Exodus 12:1 – 2.

2. On the 14th day which is four days later, all the people of Israel must slaughter the animals at twilight, Exodus 12:6.

3. Next, the Israelites will place some of the blood on the sides and tops of the doorposts of the house where they are eating the lamb, Exodus 12:7.

4. On the same night, the Israelites will eat the meat roasted over the fire, along with bitter herbs, and bread made without yeast; anything left over must be burned by morning, Exodus 12:8.

5. The Israelites are commanded to eat with their cloak tucked into their belts, and their sandals should be on their feet and their staff in their hand. They are to eat in haste; it's the Lord's Passover, Exodus 12:11.

Note of Interests: The Jewish people customarily take off their shoes and sandals during meals, Luke 7:36 – 38, John 13:1 – 5; but the Jews are commanded to wear sandals on their feet at the Passover, Exodus 12:11.

~~~~~~~~~~~~

The Passover Celebration is mentioned throughout the Bible.

1. In Numbers 9, the Israelites celebrate the Passover in the wilderness.
2. In Joshua 5, Joshua celebrated the Passover after bringing the Israelites into the Promised Land.
3. In 2 Chronicles 30, the Passover is observed during the reign of King Hezekiah.
4. In 2 Kings 23, the Passover is celebrated during the reign of King Josiah.

5. In Ezra 6, when the Israelites returned to Jerusalem from Babylonian captivity, they observed the Passover.

6. And in the New Testament, Jesus shared the Passover meal with his disciples before he was arrested, beaten, and crucified; Matthew 26, Mark 14, Luke 22, and John 13.

Chapter 5

THY SHOES

Deuteronomy 33:25

"**Thy shoes** shall be iron and brass; and as
thy days, so shall thy strength be." KJV

~~~

The verse typed above is embedded in the Book of
Deuteronomy. Deuteronomy is considered the last Book of
the Law, written by Moses. The other 4 Books of the Law
are Genesis, Exodus, Leviticus, and Numbers.

The Book of Deuteronomy is the 5th book of the Old
Testament, and it contains 34 chapters. In chapters 1 – 30,
there are 3 speeches, some scholars call them sermons which
Moses delivered to the Israelites on the plains of Moab,
shortly before they enter the Promised Land.

The 1st speech recounts the 40 years of wilderness wandering
and urges the Israelites to observe the law. The 2nd speech
reminds the Israelites of the need to obey the Lord's laws
because their possession of the land depends upon it. The
3rd speech states, if Israel becomes unfaithful to the Lord,
and lose the land if they repent, the Lord will restore them.

The last 4 chapters of Deuteronomy contain the Song of Moses, the blessing that Moses pronounced over the Israelites, Joshua as his successor, and the death of Moses on Mount Nebo. In the 33rd chapter of Deuteronomy is where Moses is speaking blessing over the people of the 12 tribes before his death.

The 33rd chapter of Deuteronomy can be outlined as follow:

Moses Blesses the People	verses 1 – 5
Reuben's Blessing	verse 6
Judah's Blessing	verse 7
Levi's Blessing	verses 8 – 11
Benjamin's Blessing	verse 12
Joseph's Blessing	verses 13 – 17
Zebulun and Issachar's Blessing	verses 18 – 19
Gad's Blessing	verses 20 – 21
Dan's Blessing	verse 22
Naphtali's Blessing	verse 23
Asher's Blessing	verses 24 – 25
Moses Gives Praise to God	verses 26 – 29

It's in Asher's blessing where the word "shoes" is mentioned. Asher's blessing reads as follow:

> **And of Asher he (Moses) said,**
> **Let Asher be blessed with children; let**
> **him be acceptable to his brethren,**
> **and let him dip his foot in oil.**

Thy shoes shall be iron and brass; and as thy days, so shall thy strength be.
Deuteronomy 33:24 – 25 KJV

Asher was the 2nd son of Jacob and Zilpah, and the father of the Tribe of Asher. His name means "happy" or "bless." Asher name is mentioned 42 times in the Bible, and only in the Old Testament.

In verse 24 of Deuteronomy 33, Moses is prophesying to Asher, telling him he will be blessed with children and they shall be numerous, strong and healthy. Moses explains to Asher, he will be acceptable by his brethren because of his pleasant disposition. Moses also told Asher that he shall have plenty of oil that he may not only wash his face but his feet, too. Asher's tribe was located on the northern seacoast which is the best area for olives to grow.

Deuteronomy 33:25 has several translations. In this verse, Moses is prophesying to Asher that the mines of iron and copper will produce a vast quantity of brass. Some scholars believe that this verse is referring to the iron and copper mines in their territory. Other scholars think it relates to their warlike disposition because ancient warriors wore greaves, boots, and shoes made from iron, brass, and tin.

Note of Interests: Goliath wore greaves of brass on his legs, 1 Samuel 17:6.

~~~~~~~~~~~~

23

The Tribe of Asher's geographical location were on the primary route of the Fertile Crescent down to Egypt. Therefore, if Asher were invaded, the whole land would be captured by a southerly invasion. Asher was considered the door to the Promised Land.

Note of Interests: The Fertile Crescent is a region that is shaped like a quarter-moon. In that region agriculture and early human civilization flourished due to the surrounding Nile, Euphrates, and Tigris Rivers. It covers Israel, Lebanon, Jordan, Syria, northern Egypt (also called lower Egypt, the region closer to the Mediterranean Sea and the Nile Delta), and Iraq. This area is also known as the "Cradle of Civilization" where many technological innovations were developed, including writing, the wheel, agriculture and the use of irrigation.

~~~~~~~~~~~~

The remainder of the prophecy to Asher is telling him his strength shall not be diminished with age, but he shall have the vigor of youth even in his old age. Asher's tribe shall grow stronger and stronger.

Note of Interests: After the Exodus, Asher totaled 41,500 men of fighting age. Forty years later, when they entered the Promised Land, Asher had reached 53,400 men of fighting age. If you compare Numbers 1:40 – 41 to Numbers 26:47 that's a "blessed increase" of 62%. According to Numbers 1:3, the fighting age begins at age 20.

~~~~~~~~~~~~

Chapter 6

OLD SHOES

Joshua 9:5
Joshua 9:13

The Book of Joshua is the 6th book in the King James Bible. It was written by Joshua between 1405 – 1383 BC. Joshua name means "a savior, a deliverer." Joshua recorded details of countless victorious military battles in central, southern, and northern Canaan against the inhabitants by the nation of Israel.

The Book of Joshua contains 24 chapters and can be divided into 3 sections. First, it describes the 7 years of conquest of the land of Canaan in chapters 1 – 11 of Joshua. Afterward, the conquered territory was divided among the tribes of Israel is outlined in Joshua, chapters 12 – 22. The assembling of the nation of Israel, Joshua' last appeal and exhortation, Joshua's death and burial is mentioned in the last two chapters of Joshua, chapters 23 and 24.

The first chapter of Joshua begins with the Lord speaking to Joshua, the son of Nun, after the death of Moses. It involved the passing of the mantle of authority from Moses to Joshua to lead the Israelites, Joshua 1:1 – 9. The nation of Israel at this time is gathered at the banks of the Jordan River poised for battle.

Note of Interests: Joshua went from slavery in Egypt to freedom in the wilderness with his people. According to Number 11:28, Joshua was Moses' servant from his youth, and eventually became the leader of the nation when they entered the Promised Land around the age of 82. Joshua was a leader of the nation of Israel for 28 years and died at the age of 110.

~~~~~~~~~~~~

The 9th chapter of Joshua has 27 verses and describes how the Gibeonites deceived Israel into making a peace treaty with them. The 5th and 13th verses of Joshua 9 are related to this deception and mentioned the word "shoes."

Joshua 9:5 reads, "And **old shoes** and clouted upon their feet, and old garments upon them; and all the bread of their provision was dry and moldy."

Joshua 9:13 reads, "And these bottles of wine, which we filled, were new; and, behold, they be rent: and these our garments and our **shoes are become old** by reason of the very long journey."

Note of Interests: The Gibeonites were the people in Gibeon who occupied the Promised Land before the arrival of the Israelites. They were descended from the Amorites and Hivites. The Amorites and Hivites were the descendants of Canaan, the son of Ham, who is the son of Noah, Genesis 10:15. Ham other sons were named Cush, Egypt, and Put,

Genesis 10:6. Noah's sons were Shem, Ham, and Japheth, 1 Chronicles 1:4.

~~~~~~~~~~~~

The beginning of Joshua 9 mentioned that the kings of the Hittites, Amorites, Canaanites, Perizzites, Hivites, and Jebusites combined their armies to fight as one against Joshua and the Israelites when they heard how Joshua and his army defeated Jericho and Ai.

When the Gibeonites heard how Joshua and his army defeated Jericho and Ai, they approached Joshua and the Israelites in another manner. They worked in deception, instead of warfare with Israel. The Gibeonites pretended to be ambassadors from far away. The Gibeonites placed old sacks on their donkeys, along with old wineskins. They wore patched shoes/sandals on their feet and old garments on themselves, Joshua 9:5. They took bread with them that was old and moldy as part of their deception.

The Gibeonites went to Israel's camp at Gilgal. They told Joshua and the men of Israel that they had come from a far country and wanted to make a peace treaty with them. The men of Israel told them they didn't want to make a treaty with anyone that lived near them. When Joshua asked them where they come from, they lied. They told Joshua they had heard of his God and all He had done in Egypt and to the two kings of the Amorites, Sihon the king of Heshbon, and Og the king of Bashan.

The Gibeonites also told Joshua that the elders of their land sent them on this journey. The elders told them to take provisions and meet with you, and said, "that we are your servants and please make a treaty with us."

The Gibeonites then showed Joshua the dry and moldy bread, the wineskins which were cracked, old raggedy clothes and shoes/sandals that they claim had worn out on their very long journey, Joshua 9:13.

The Israelites examined these items but did not seek the Lord counsel. Joshua made a peace treaty with them, and the leaders of Israel agreed. Three days after making the treaty with the Gibeonites, the Israelites learned that they were living near them. So, the Israelites set out and on the 3rd day arrived at their cities; Gibeon, Kephirah, Beeroth, and Kiriath Jearim.

The Israelites did not attack the Gibeonites' cities because they had sworn an oath to them by the Lord, the God of Israel. The leaders explained to Israel because they had given them their oath, Israel would have to allow the Gibeonites to live so that God's wrath wouldn't fall on Israel for breaking the oath that was sworn to them.

The Gibeonites deceived Israel into making a peace treaty with them, even though Israel was forbidden by the Lord to make peace with any of the tribes of the land of Canaan, Exodus 23:23 – 24.

Joshua wouldn't allow them to be killed. He made the Gibeonites the woodcutters and water carriers for the altar of the Lord. So, the treaty was kept. The Gibeonites are woodcutters and water carriers to this day.

Note of Interests: When Saul became king, he broke this peace treaty with the Gibeonites, and it brought famine upon the land of Israel for 3 years, 2 Samuel 21:1. In order, to end this famine, 7 sons of Saul were given to the Gibeonites to be put to death, and then God healed Israel's land afterward, 2 Samuel 21:6 – 14.

~~~~~~~~~~~~

Chapter 7

IN HIS SHOES

1 Kings 2:5

The final words of King David to his son, Solomon:

Moreover, thou knowest also went Joab the son of Zeruiah did to me, and what he did to the two captains of the hosts of Israel, unto Abner the son of Ner, and unto Amasa the son of Jether, whom he slew, and shed the blood of war in peace, and put the blood of war upon his girdle that was about his loins, and **in his shoes** that were on his feet. KJV

~~~

The books of 1st and 2nd Kings were initially one book; they are now the 11th and 12th books of the Old Testament. 1st and 2nd Kings are the last two books of "Deuteronomistic History." The other Deuteronomistic History books are Joshua, Judges, 1st and 2nd Samuel.

The Deuteronomistic History is the history of Israel that provides a biblical explanation for the destruction of the Kingdom of Judah by Babylon in 586 BC and shows the steps for the return of Israel from exile. The books of Kings present a history of ancient Israel and Judah from the death of

King David to the release of Jehoiachin from imprisonment in Babylon, a period of some 400 years; 960 – 560 BC.

Note of Interests: ehoiachin was a young Israelite king who is also referred to as Jeconiah and Coniah. He was only 8 years old when he begins his reign, 2 Chronicles 36:9 KJV. Recorded in NIV and NLT of 2 Chronicles 36:9, Jehoiachin was 18 years old when he begins his reign. He ruled in Judah for 3 months and 10 days before he was dethroned by the King of Babylon and taken into captivity around 597 BC.

~~~~~~~~~~~

However, 1ˢᵗ Kings, chapter 2 is concerning King David's last words to his son, Solomon, verses 1 - 9. At this particular time, Israel was still one nation. As time drew near for David to die, he called Solomon and gave him some instructions. King David told Solomon that he is about to die, as everyone must do on this earth. He tells Solomon he wants him to be strong, take courage and be a man.

David stressed to his son to walk in obedience and follow the teaching of the Lord; the God of Israel. David tells Solomon to keep the commandments, statutes, rules, and commands as it is written in the Law of Moses, so that he may prosper and be successful in everything he does, and wherever he goes. If he carefully obeys the Lord's commands faithfully with all his heart and soul, the Lord will keep his solemn promise that someone from their family will always be the king of Israel, 1 Kings 2:4.

Note of Interests: Commandments, Statutes, Rules, and Commands are various words repeatedly used in the Bible. The word commandment usually refers to the laws given to Moses by the Lord, Exodus 20. The statutes apply to laws of nature, for example, Job 28:26, Jeremiah 5:22, Jeremiah 31:35, 36. Rules are formal decrees, which are official orders issued by a legal authority. The Commands refer to a law related to a festival or ritual; the Passover, the Days of Unleavened Bread, the Feast of Tabernacles, Exodus 12:14, Exodus 12:17 and Leviticus 23:41.

~~~~~~~~~~~~

The next verse, 1 Kings 2:5 has 73 words and consist of 7 commas, KJV. The words "in his shoes" is embedded in this verse. King David tells Solomon don't forget what Joab, the son of Zeruiah did. He killed Abner, son of Ner and Amasa, son of Jether. They were 2 mighty commanders of Israel's army. Joab killed them during the time of peace to avenge the blood of war. David tells Solomon that Joab spilled their blood on his belt about his waist, and on his shoes, that's on his feet. David tells Solomon that Joab killed innocent men, and he is guilty of murder, and now it's up to him to punish him. King David tells Solomon to use wisdom, don't let him live long, nor have a peaceful death.

King David also tells Solomon in verse 7, to show kindness and be loyal to the sons of Barzillai the Gileadite. Barzillai helped King David when he fled from his rebellion son, Absalom. Barzillai was 80 years old, and he provided for the king during his stay in Mahanaim, 2 Samuel 19:32. The Gileadites brought wheat, barley, flour, roasted grain, beans, lentils, honey, curds, sheep, cheese, and milk for David and his people to eat, when they were in the wilderness, 2 Samuel 17:27 – 29.

Also, in 1 Kings 2, King David tells Solomon to keep an eye on Shimei the son of Gera, the Benjamite from Bahurim who utter bitter curses against him on the day he went to Mahanaim. When Shimei came down to meet King David at the Jordan River, King David swore to him in the name of the Lord that he wouldn't have him killed. King David tells Solomon that he must punish him by putting him to death.

Verse 10 of 1 King 2, tells us that David rested with his fathers and was buried in the City of David. Verses 11, records that David's reign 40 years over Israel; 7 years in Hebron and 33 years in Jerusalem. Verse 12, states that Solomon sat on the throne of his father David, and his rule was firmly established.

The next section of this chapter, verses 13 – 46 is Solomon establishing his reign.

Solomon had Benaiah to kill his brother, Adonijah, vs. 13 – 25.
Solomon decided not to kill Abiathar the priest, vs. 26 – 27.
Solomon had Benaiah to kill Joab, vs. 28 – 35.
Solomon had Shimei killed 3 years later by Benaiah, vs. 36 – 46.

Take a moment, and read 1 King 2 in its entirety . . .
You'll be enlightened.

Chapter 8

FEET WITH SHOES

Song of Solomon 7:1

How beautiful are thy **feet with shoes**, O prince's daughter! The joints of thy thighs are like jewels, the work of the hands of a cunning workman. KJV

How beautiful your **sandaled feet**, O prince's daughter! Your graceful legs are like jewels, the work of an artist's hands. NIV

How beautiful are your **sandaled feet**, O queenly maiden. Your rounded thighs are like jewels, the work of a skilled craftsman. NLT

~~~

The 22nd book of the Old Testament is called Song of Songs. The title "Song of Songs" is a Hebrew expression which means "The Best Songs." Song of Songs consists of only 8 chapters. It is also known as Song of Solomon because King Solomon name is mentioned 6 times in the book; Song of Songs 1:5; 3:7; 3:9, 3:11, 8:11 and 8:12. According to 1 Kings

4:32, Solomon composed 1,005 songs and spoke over 3,000 proverbs.

Solomon wrote Song of Songs during his reign as king of Israel; therefore, it was written between 971 and 931 BC. Scholars who believe that Solomon wrote Song of Songs agree that the book was written early in his reign, because of the youthful exuberance of the poetry and the mention of only 140 women, Song of Songs 6:8. According to 1 Kings 11:3, Solomon had 700 wives and 300 concubines.

Song of Songs stands out because of its beautiful detailed vision of courtship and marriage. The entire book pertains to romance, affection, desire and marital love. The words and thoughts of 2 people in love, praising and yearning for each other is written in these 8 chapters. Jewish tradition believes Song of Songs is an allegory between God and Israel, while Christianity believes it is an allegory of Christ and his bride; the Church.

Note of Interests: An "allegory" can be a story, poem or painting that can be interpreted to reveal a hidden meaning or another message. It could also be a story in which people, things, or happenings have a symbolic meaning. The characters or message often symbolize a concept or idea from real life.

~~~~~~~~~~~~

Song of Songs begins with Solomon describing a relationship with two lovers in courtship. They are longing for each other affection while expressing their love for one another, Song of

Songs 1:1 – 3:5. Eventually, they come together in marriage. The groom describes and admires his bride's beauty before they consummate their relationship, Song of Songs 3:6 – 5:1. Finally, she struggles with the fear of losing him. The groom reassures his bride of his true affections for her, Song of Songs 5:2 – 8:14. Many Scholars believe the Song of Songs is a picture of Christ's love for His bride, the church.

Chapter 7 of Song of Songs has 13 verses, verses 1 – 9 is more description of the beautiful young woman. Her beauty is also described in Song of Songs 4:1 – 7 and 6:4 – 10. Song of Songs 7 is different from Song of Songs 4 and 6 because it describes her lower body compared to chapters 4 and 6, where he only describes her head and her breasts.

In Song of Songs 7, Solomon describes her feet looking graceful in her sandals; her thighs are works of art, Song of Songs 7:1. Solomon goes on to describe her navel. He describes her body as slender as a bundle of wheat. He mentioned that her breasts are like twins of a deer, and her neck is like ivory, while her eyes sparkle like the pools of Heshbon. Solomon states her nose is beautiful like Mount Lebanon, and her head is held high like Mount Carmel. She is tall and slender like a palm tree, and her breasts are full, and her kisses are more delicious than the finest wine, Song of Songs 7:2 – 9.

Scholar believes, before chapter 7 of Song of Songs, the groom did not consider it proper to describe her lower body. When she became his wife, he then had the right to do so. Before chapter 7, she wore a veil to cover her face, but after the marriage, she allowed him to see her without a veil. Everything that he sees is beautiful.

According to verse 6, he completes his last description of his wife. She is lovely and pleases him completely. In the last 3 verses of Solomon 7, the new wife gives her husband an invitation. Scholars believe these words to his spouse is Christ's words to the church. She is responding to her husband/Christ's words of love in the previous verses. She is victorious in her relationship to Christ and will rejoice and talk about her love for him all day. In verse 10, she said, "I am my beloved's, not my own, but entirely devoted to him and owned by him." She ends chapter 7 by saying, "come, my beloved, let us take a walk together, that she may receive counsel, instruction, and comfort from thee, and may make known her wants and grievance to thee, with freedom and without interruption, Song of Songs 7:11 – 12.

The last verse of Song of Songs reads:

There the mandrakes give off their fragrance,
and the finest fruits are at our door,
new delights as well as old which I have saved for you,
my lover.
Song of Songs 7:13 NLT

Note of Interests: Mandrake is a flowering plant which resembles a potato. It is found buried underground with its flowery part above ground. They are noted for their roots, which resemble the human form. In Bible days, mandrake roots were considered an aphrodisiac. It was prepared and eaten to enhance a woman conception.

Mandrakes are mentioned in many folklores, but mandrakes are only mentioned 6 times in 2 biblical events in the Bible; Genesis 30 and Song of Solomon 7. According to Genesis 30, Jacob was married to 2 sisters named Rachel and Leah. Rachel was childless, and Leah had 4 sons. Reuben, the son of Leah, found some mandrakes in the field and gave them to his mother. Leah then trades them with Rachel in exchange for the opportunity to sleep with Jacob that night, Genesis 30:14 – 16. Rachel accepts the trade, believing that the mandrakes would help her conceive. Leah slept with Jacob that night and became pregnant with her 5th son, Issachar.

~~~~~~~~~~~~

Chapter 9

SHOES BE BROKEN

Isaiah 5:27

None shall be weary nor stumble among them; none shall slumber nor sleep; neither shall the girdle of their loins be loosed, nor the latchet of their **shoes be broken**: KJV

~~~

The Book of Isaiah is the 1st book of the 5 Major Prophet Books in the Old Testament Bible; Jeremiah, Lamentations, Ezekiel, and Daniel are the other 4 books. The Book of Isaiah is considered one of the most important books of the Old Testament. It's a collection of oracles, prophecies, reports, and the message of salvation.

The Book of Isaiah has 66 chapters. It was written approximately 700 BC; chapters 40 – 66 is believed by Scholars to have been written around 681 BC. Old Testament Scholars believe several different authors produced the book.

Isaiah chapters 1 – 39 are entirely different and distinct from chapters 40 – 66. Prophet Isaiah is given credit for writing chapters 1 – 39 of Isaiah. Those chapters deal mainly with

Judah and Jerusalem when the city was still standing but was threatened by the Assyrians' invasion. Chapters 40 – 66 appears to have been written about Israel conditions that prevailed more than a century later. In this section, the writer mentioned the Babylonian captivity has existed for a long time. These chapters also mentioned the future for God's people, Israelites.

The Book of Isaiah was named after Isaiah, an 8th century BC Jewish Prophet. His name means "The Lord is Salvation." Isaiah was a prophet of the southern kingdom. He received his call to a prophetic life in the year that King Uzziah died, 740 BC. Uzziah was one of Judah's greatest kings. He reigned approximately 50 years, and during this time, the kingdom enjoyed a period of prosperity. Isaiah was married to a prophetess who bore him two sons, and their names were Shearjashub and Mahershalalhashbaz; Isaiah 7:3 and Isaiah 8:3.

Note of Interests: There are 9 other women in the Bible who are called a prophetess. They are Miriam, Huldah, Noahdiah, Deborah, Anna and Philip's 4 daughters. Other women in the Bible who prophesied but were not titled a prophetess were Rachel, Abigail, Hannah, Elisabeth and Mary, the mother of Jesus.

~~~~~~~~~~~~

According to Isaiah 1:1, the Prophet Isaiah's proclamation extended through the reigns of 4 kings in the southern kingdom of Judah. God showed Isaiah visions about what would happen to Judah and Jerusalem soon.

Let's name the 4 kings . . . *think and smile*

1. Uzz __ __ __
2. J__ __ h __ __
3. Ahaz
4. H__ z __ __ __ __ __

Answer in the back of the book

The 66 chapters of the Book of Isaiah can be divided as follow:

1. Chapters 1 – 39, Isaiah points out the sins of the Northern and Southern Kingdom. He declares the severe punishment that was coming to them.
2. Chapters 40 – 55, Isaiah speaks of the return and restoration after the exile from Babylon. He also foretells the coming Messiah, Isaiah 53:7.
3. Chapter 56 – 66, Isaiah wrote about the new Heavens and Earth. The great reward for all who trust and obey God, Isaiah 65:17.

The 5th chapter of Isaiah is where the word "shoes" is mentioned, and it can be outlined as follow:

1. A Song about the Lord's Vineyard Destroyed, verses 1 – 7
2. Isaiah's Woe to the Wicked, verses 8 – 25
3. God will Bring Foreign Nations to Punish Israel, verses 26 – 30

The subject title, "God will Bring Foreign Nations to Punish Israel" is where the 27th verse is embedded. Beginning at verse 26, God had signalled the foreign far away nations to attack Israel. The 27th verse states that these warriors don't get tired, or stumble. They don't even stop for rest or sleep. The 2nd part of this verse is where the word "shoes" is mentioned. It states that the soldiers' belt will not become loose, and the latchet of their shoes are unbroken.

The remainder of chapter 5 describes the warriors and the outcome of the battle. They will have sharp arrows, and all their bows will be ready for battle. The horses' hoofs are hard as flint, and the wheels of their war chariots spin fast like a whirlwind.

The warriors roar and growl like fierce young lions as they seize their victims. There will be no one to rescue Israel from them. On the day, the foreign warriors attack, they will roar like the vast sea. They will come across the land, and Israel will see nothing but darkness because thick clouds will cover the light of day.

When God's word is despised, his laws cast away, and people will not listen to the Prophet, men can expect God's wrath. God decided this destruction on Israel because they were disobedient. He utilizes nations to render his wrath. God sent for the Assyrian, and afterward the Romans to destroy the Jews. When people do not listen to the voice of God speaking through his prophets, they shall hear their enemies roaring against them.

Chapter 10

SHOES UPON THY FEET

Ezekiel 24:17
Ezekiel 24:23

Forbear to cry, make no mourning for the dead, bind the tire of thine head upon thee, and put on thy **shoes upon thy feet**, and cover not thy lips, and eat not the bread of men. Ezekiel 24:17 KJV

And your tires shall be upon your heads, and your **shoes upon your feet**: ye shall not mourn nor weep; but ye shall pine away for your iniquities and mourn one toward another. Ezekiel 24:23 KJV

~~~

Ezekiel was one of the younger men among the Hebrews exiled to Babylon by Nebuchadnezzar in the first captivity which occurred in 597 BC. His name means "God strengthens." Ezekiel was from the tribe of Levi, the family of Aaron. There among the exiles, he received his call to become a prophet.

The Book of Ezekiel opens with an account of the visions that summoned Ezekiel to his prophetic calling. There he describes his visions, proclaims the Lord's sovereignty over all the nations of the earth, fell on his face, and heard a voice. The voice said to him, "Son of man, I am sending you to the children of Israel, to a rebellious nation that has rebelled against me, Ezekiel 2:3.

According to Ezekiel 3, Ezekiel is handed a scroll to eat and the words lament, mourning, and pronouncements of doom are written on it," Ezekiel 3:1 – 3. Ezekiel's mission is to prophesy an impending disaster against the people of Israel.

Ezekiel became a priest-prophet called to minister to his people who were permitted to live in a Babylonian colony near the banks of the Kebar River while in exile. Ezekiel lived in a house of his own, and his fellow exiles visit him, Ezekiel 3:24 and Ezekiel 8:1. Even though they were confined to Babylon, they had a relatively free existence there.

The Book of Ezekiel has 48 chapters. Scholars believe that Ezekiel wrote the entire book while living in the colony of the exiles between 593 and 565 BC. This colony was about 400 miles from Jerusalem. The Book of Ezekiel is a book of visions, oracles, and symbolic acts surrounded by 3 subject matters:

1. The Fall of Jerusalem and Judgment on Israel, chapters 1 – 24
2. Oracles and Judgment on the Foreign Nations, chapters 25 – 32

3. Plan for Rebuilding the Temple and Restoring Israel, chapters 33 – 48

The 24th chapter of Ezekiel contains the last message of God before the fall of Jerusalem. The fall of Jerusalem is dated, January 15, 588 BC; 2 Kings 25:1, Jeremiah 39:1, and Jeremiah 52:4. This date was memorialized among the captives, as a ceremonial fast-day.

Note of Interests: Fast-day or fasting is the abstinence from food and/or water. It is an individual devotion which can be private or collective religious devotion. Fasting is connected to several significant events in the Bible regards to life experiences which are lamentation, repentance, mourning, and petition. The 1st act of fasting is recorded in Judges 20:21 – 28, after a war between Israel and Benjamin. Joel called the people to fast twice, Joel 1:14, Joel 2:15. People of Jabesh-Gilead fasted after Saul death, 1 Samuel 31:13, along with David, 2 Samuel 1:12. David fasted over his sick child, 2 Samuel 12:16. Nehemiah wept and fasted after hearing about Jerusalem desolation, Nehemiah 1:4 – 11. Esther urged Mordecai and the Jews to fast as she prepares to go before her husband, the king, Esther 4:16. The Prophetess Anna looked for the redemption of Israel with supplicatory prayer and fasting, Luke 2:37. Jesus fasted 40 days and nights, Matthew 4. The disciples fasted before they appointed Barnabas and Saul to do the work of the Lord, Acts 13:1 – 3. Before Paul and Barnabas appointed elders for the churches, they committed them to the Lord with prayer and fasting, Acts 14:23.

~~~~~~~~~~~

The Book of Ezekiel, chapter 24 has 3 sections:

1. The Siege of Jerusalem, verses 1 – 14
2. Ezekiel's Wife Death, verses 15 – 24
3. Ezekiel will Speak, verses 25 – 27

According to Ezekiel 24, the Prophet Ezekiel was married. At the fall of Jerusalem, two dramatic incidents occurred on the same day. The siege of Jerusalem and the death of Ezekiel's wife.

Ezekiel was told that his wife would die by the Lord. The Lord instructed Ezekiel that he was forbidden to make any visible demonstration of his grief. All of the customary acts that were usually performed to mark the passing of a loved one were to be omitted.

Ezekiel head would remain covered, his sandals/shoes wouldn't be taken off, he couldn't go barefoot, nor could he mourn or weep aloud, nor could he console himself by eating food brought by his friends, Ezekiel 24:15 – 17. Ezekiel 24, verses 17 and 23 is where the words "shoes upon thy feet" are embedded. Usually, during the time of mourning, shoes are removed from your feet.

According to Ezekiel 24:20 – 23, Ezekiel is answering a question by the people. Ezekiel's wife had died, and they asked him why isn't he mourning for his wife? Ezekiel responded to the question with the instructions the Lord gave him in verses 15 – 17.

Note of Interests: The funeral customs that the Lord instructed Ezekiel not to do are frequently mentioned in the Old Testament. Many are mentioned in the New Testament, as in the case of the loud mourners wailing for the death of Jairus' daughter, and the death of Lazarus; Luke 8 and John 11.

~~~~~~~~~~~~

Chapter 11

FOR A PAIR OF SHOES

Amos 2:6

Amos 8:6

Thus, saith the Lord; For three transgressions of Israel, and for four, I will not turn away the punishment thereof; because they sold the righteous for silver, and the poor **for a pair of shoes**; Amos 2:6 KJV.

That we may buy the poor for silver, and the needy **for a pair of shoes**; yea, and sell the refuse of the wheat? Amos 8:6 KJV

~~~

The Book of Amos is the 30th book of the Old Testament. It is the 3rd book of the 12 Minor Prophet Books in the Old Testament. Amos is the author, and he wrote it between the years of 760 and 750 BC. The Book of Amos has 9 chapters of oracles. The book was written at a time of peace and prosperity, but Israel was neglecting the Lord's laws.

Let's name the other Minor Prophet Books.
You can do it!

   1. H_____
   2. J_____
   3. Amos
   4. O_____
   5. J_____
   6. Mi_____
   7. N_____
   8. H_____
   9. Zep_____
 10. Haggai
 11. Z_____
 12. Ma_____

Answer in the back of the book

Amos lived in the Southern Kingdom of Israel called Judah, but his prophetic mission was in the Northern Kingdom of Israel where he announced God's future judgment on the Northern Kingdom.

Note of Interests: The Southern Kingdom consisted of 2 tribes which were Benjamin and Judah. The Northern Kingdom of Israel consisted of 10 tribes which were Reuben, Simeon, Manasseh, Issachar, Zebulun, Ephraim, Dan, Asher, Naphtali, and Gad.

~~~~~~~~~~~~

Amos was from Tekoa, a small town in Judah about 6 miles south of Bethlehem and 11 miles from Jerusalem. Amos was not a prophet but a holy man who attended sheep, but God sent him with a message to His people, Israel. Amos is called a shepherd and a dresser of sycamore trees, Amos 7:14 – 15. Amos was an older contemporary of Hosea and Isaiah around 750 BC during the reign of Jeroboam II, making the Book of Amos the 1st biblical prophetic book written.

When Amos produce was ready for market, he traveled through towns, villages, and the cities of Israel. He observed the hardships placed on the working class of people by the wealthy landowners who lived in prosperity. Amos was deeply troubled by the difference between the wealth and poor lifestyle.

As Amos thought on the poor and their living conditions in Northern Israel, he began to see visions; a total of 5 which are listed below.

First Vision:
Locusts.
Amos saw a swarm of locusts devouring the produce of the land. This vision represents the destruction of the harvest in the days that lie ahead, Amos 7:1 – 3.

Second Vision:
Fire.
Amos saw the Sovereign Lord call judgment by fire, and it dried up the depth of the sea, and devoured the land, Amos 7:4 – 6.

Third Vision:
Plumbline.

Amos saw a man with a plumbline measuring a wall about to collapse. The wall symbolizes the house of Israel. The nation of Israel will soon collapse and go into captivity, Amos 7:7 – 9.

Fourth Vision:

Basket of Ripe Fruit.

Amos saw a basket of ripe fruit which represents the people of Israel's material possession, but ripe fruit only lasts for a little while before it spoils. The peaceful and prosperous years of the Israelites are coming to an end, Amos 8.

Fifth Vision:

The Lord.

Amos saw the Lord standing by the altar.

The Book of Amos can be outlined as follow:

Chapters 1 – 3, The people of the Northern Kingdom were religious, but it was only superficial. Amos announces that the nearby wicked nations would be punished, including Damascus, Gaza, Edom, and Tyre.

Chapters 4 – 8, Amos warns Israel that they would be destroyed. He announces God's coming judgment to the Northern Kingdom, and the Assyrians would eventually exile them.

Chapter 9, Amos tells of the restoration and hope of Israel. The Lord said, "In that day I will raise up the fallen booth of David and wall up its breaches; I will also raise up its ruins and rebuild it as in the days of old."

Chapter 2 of Amos is where the word "shoes" is first mentioned in the Book of Amos, then in chapter 8 of Amos. The 2nd chapter of Amos can be outlined as follow:

1. God's Judgments upon Moab, verses 1 – 3
2. God's Judgments upon Judah, verses 4 – 5
3. God's Judgments upon Israel, verses 6 – 8
4. God Complains about their Ingratitude, verses 9 – 16

Beginning at Amos 2:6, the Lord said, "He will punish Israel for their countless crimes, and He won't change his mind. They have sinned repeatedly. They have sold honest people for money, and the people who are in need are sold for the price of a pair of shoes/sandals. They trample the helpless and push aside the oppressed. The father and son both sleep with the same woman, disgracing his holy name. They drink wine in the temple bought with unjust fines, verses 7 and 8.

The 8th chapter of Amos consists of 14 verses. Verses 1 – 3, the Lord showed Amos a basket of ripe fruit. In verses 4 – 10, the Lord tells Amos Israel is doomed, and he explained why. In verses 11 – 14, the Lord promises Israel a famine over the land, but not of bread or water but a famine of hearing the words of the Lord.

The 6th verse of Amos 8 is repeating what Amos 2:6 stated. The Lord is speaking to Amos, and he is giving the reasons he is about to punish Israel. One of the reasons is verse 6.

**And you mix grain you sell with
chaff swept from the floor.
Then you enslave poor people for one piece of silver or
a pair of sandals.**
Amos 8:6 NLT

Chapter 12

WHOSE SHOES

Matthew 3:11
Mark 1:7
Luke 3:16
John 1:27
Acts 13:25

I indeed baptize you with water unto repentance. But he that cometh after me is mightier than I, **whose shoes** I am not worthy to bear: he shall baptize you with the Holy Ghost, and with fire. Matthew 3:11 KJV

And preaching, saying, There cometh one mightier than I after me, the latchets of **whose shoes** I am not worthy to stoop down and unloose. Mark 1:7 KJV

John answered, saying unto them all, I indeed baptize you with water; but one mightier than I cometh, the latchet of **whose shoes** I am not worthy to unloose: he shall baptize you with the Holy Ghost and with fire. Luke 3:16 KJV

He it is, who coming after me is preferred before me, **whose shoe's** latchet I am not worthy to unloose. John 1:27 KJV

And as John fulfilled his course, he said, Whom think ye that I am? I am not he. But, behold, there cometh one after me, **whose shoes** of his feet I am not worthy to loose. Acts 13:25 KJV

~~~

The exact words **"whose shoes"** are recorded in the gospels of Matthew, Mark, Luke, John and the Book of Acts. These are the words of John the Baptist recorded in 5 books of the Bible in the New Testament.

The Gospel of Matthew has 28 chapters. It was written by Matthew, one of the 12 disciples of Jesus, who later became an Apostle. He was also known as Levi, the tax collector who left everything to follow Jesus. The Gospel of Matthew was written between 80 and 90 AD. In the 3rd chapter of Matthew is where the words "whose shoes" are embedded. This chapter only has 17 verses. Jesus' forerunner, John the Baptist is described in verses 1 – 12, and Jesus' baptism is mentioned in verses 13 – 17.

John the Baptist is preparing the way for Jesus' ministry. He was preaching in the wilderness of Judea. He was telling the crowd of people to repent for the kingdom of heaven has come near. The man who cometh after him is mightier than he, whose shoes he is not worthy to bear, and he shall baptize them with the Holy Ghost, and with fire, Matthew 3:11.

The Gospel of Mark has 16 chapters. Most scholars credit John Mark as the writer of this gospel. They believe it was written around 66 – 70 AD.

The 1st chapter of Mark has 45 verses, and the 7th verse is where the words "whose shoes" is mentioned. It reads, "the latchet of whose shoes I am not worthy to stoop down and unloose," while Matthew 3 reads, "whose shoes I am not worthy to bear." In both verses, the phrase "whose shoes I am not worthy" is stressed; the rest of the phrase has different wordings but give the same concept.

Mark begins his gospel with John the Baptist preparing the way for Jesus, Mark 1. He was preaching and baptizing in the wilderness, verses 1 – 8. John the Baptist preached that after him comes he who is mightier than him, the latchet of whose shoes he was not worthy to stoop down and unloose.

The remainder of this chapter, verses 9 – 45, speaks on the baptism and testing of Jesus. It also mentions John the Baptist place in prison. It tells us that Jesus proclaims the good news, calls his 1st disciples, drives out an unclean spirit in a man, heals many, along with Simon's wife mother. Afterward, Jesus prays in a solitary place, and heals a man with leprosy.

The Gospel of Luke has 24 chapters. Luke was a Gentile physician by trade who never met Jesus but became a follower of Jesus. He was a faithful traveling companion of Paul. He was with Paul at the time of his martyrdom in Rome, 2 Timothy 4:11.

Luke also wrote the Book of Acts which he addressed it to the most honorable Theophilus, so he can be certain of the truth of everything he was taught, Luke 1:1 – 4, Acts 1:1 – 2.

The 3rd chapter of Luke has 38 verses. In the 16th verse is where "whose shoes" are mentioned. Luke begins chapter 3 with the year, and who was reigning during the time of John the Baptist's preaching. It was in the 15th year during the reign of Tiberias Caesar, and Pontius Pilate was the governor of Judea, and Herod was the governor of Galilee. Luke also in this chapter mentioned the baptism of Jesus, recorded that Jesus was about 30 years old at this time and listed his genealogy.

Luke stated the people were being baptized, excited and wondered was John the Baptist, the Messiah. Luke 3:16 recorded the answer John gave them: "John answered, saying unto them all, I indeed baptize you with water; but one mightier than I cometh, the latchet of whose shoes I am not worthy to unloose: he shall baptize you with the Holy Ghost and with fire." KJV

The Gospel of John has 21 chapters, and it was written by John, "the beloved disciple" of Jesus; not John the Baptist. His gospel recounts the life, ministry, death, and resurrection of Jesus. Scholars believe it was written at Ephesus in Asia Minor, to communicate the truth about Jesus Christ. John's gospel was the last gospel to be written, and it was written near the end of the 1st century, around 98 AD.

The Gospel of John, chapter 1 has 51 verses, and it mentioned the words "whose shoes" in the 27th verse. John begins the chapter with, "In the beginning was the Word, and the Word was with God, and the Word was God," John 1:1. It continues with an introduction of the deity of Jesus Christ, verses 2 – 18.

Beginning at verse 19, John's gospel gives the testimony of John the Baptist. The Jewish leaders from Jerusalem sent priests and Levites to ask John who he was.

John denied being the Christ. He replied he was the voice of the one crying out in the wilderness to, "clear the way for the Lord's is coming!"

When those sent by the Pharisee heard this, they asked John why do he baptize if he wasn't the Christ, nor Elijah, nor the prophet? John answered, saying he baptizes with water, but the one that comes after him is preferred before him, whose shoe's latchet he was not worthy to unloose, verses 24 – 27. John 1:27 reads, "Though his ministry follows mine, I'm not even worthy to be his slave and untie the straps of his sandal." NLT

The next day John seeth Jesus
coming unto him, and saith,
Behold the Lamb of God, which taketh
away the sin of the world.
John 1:29 KJV

The Book of Acts gives a detailed account of the birth, the growth of the early church, and the spread of the gospel immediately after the ascension of Jesus Christ. It consists of 28 chapters and was written by Luke.

The Book of Acts, chapter 13 has 52 verses, and verse 25 is where Paul mentioned John the Baptist's words "whose shoes." Paul and Barnabas were in Antioch of Pisidia, Acts 13:13 – 52. On the Sabbath, they went to a Jewish meeting place for worship. The leaders asked Paul and Barnabas did they have anything to say to the people to help them. Paul stood up and begin to tell the crowd how God prosper Israel's ancestor in Egypt in slavery, and down through the generations.

Beginning at verse 24 of Acts 13 is where Paul begins to speak about John the Baptist who preached to the people of Israel to turn back to God and be baptized. John the Baptist explained that he wasn't the Messiah; the Promised One, but he will come soon, whose shoes of his feet he was not worthy to loosen, Acts 13:25.

Apostle Paul goes on to speak about the people of Jerusalem, and their leaders didn't realize who Jesus was. They condemned Jesus just as the prophets of old had said. Even though they couldn't find any reason to put Jesus to death, they still plead with Pilate to have him crucified. Jesus was put to death on a cross of Calvary. When he was taken down from the cross, he was placed in a tomb, and God raised him from the dead. Afterward, Jesus appeared to his followers for many days before his ascension into heaven.

Note of Interests: Joseph, a rich man from Arimathea, had become a disciple of Jesus. He wrapped Jesus' body in a clean linen cloth and placed his body in a new tomb, Matthew 27:57 – 61. Jesus rose from the grave on the 3rd day, for 40 days he presented himself to his disciples, and others before his ascension. They are listed below:

Early Sunday Morning:
1) Mary Magdalene, John 20:16
2) Salome and Mary the Mother of James, Matthew 28:9

Sunday' Afternoon:
3) Two Disciples on the Road of Emmaus, Luke 24:13 – 32
4) Peter in Jerusalem, Luke 24:34, 1 Corinthians 15:5
5) Jesus Appeared to a Small Gathering of Apostles
6) Apostles Behind Closed Doors, except Thomas, Luke 24:36

One Week Later:
7) The Apostles with Thomas, John 20:24 – 29

Sometime Later:
8) Some of the Apostles at Sea of Galilee, who had gone fishing, John 21
9) Jesus appeared to 500, 1 Corinthians 15:6
10) Jesus appeared to James, his half-brother, 1 Corinthians 15:7

The Rest of the 40 Days:
11) Mountaintop in Galilee, Matthew 28:16 and Mark 16:14
12) Before Jesus led his disciples to a place near Bethany, He gave them instructions to stay in Jerusalem until the Holy Spirit fills them with power from heaven. Then Jesus was taken up to heaven in their very sight, Luke 24:49 – 53, Acts 1:1 – 11.

***Jesus appeared to Paul, formerly known as Saul of Tarsus, after his ascension, 1 Corinthians 15:3 – 8.

~~~~~~~~~~~~

The 13th chapter of Acts ends with the people begging Paul and Barnabas to preach on the next Sabbath. The Jewish leaders stirred up trouble when they saw the crowd of people that followed them. Paul and Barnabas shook the dust from that place off their feet and went on to the city of Iconium, Acts 13:51. The last verse of this chapter reads:

> **And the believers were filled with**
> **joy and with the Holy Spirit.**
> Acts 13:52 NLT

Chapter 13

NEITHER, NOR, WITHOUT SHOES

Matthew 10:10
Luke 10:4
Luke 22:35

Nor scrip for your journey, neither two coats, **neither shoes,** nor yet staves: for the workman is worthy of his meat. Matthew 10:10 KJV

Carry neither purse, nor scrip, **nor shoes**: and salute no man by the way. Luke 10:4 KJV

And he said unto them, When I sent you **without purse, and scrip, and shoes**, lacked ye any thing? And they said, Nothing. Luke 22:35 KJV

~~~

The verses Matthew 10:10 and Luke 10:4 are speaking on biblical events in which Jesus gave primarily the same instructions to the 72 followers, as he gave the first 12 Apostles in Matthew 10 before he sent them out to preach to the lost sheep of Israel. Luke 22:35 is a question, Jesus asked his disciples at the Last Supper.

The Gospel of Matthew and the Gospel of Luke are part of the 4 books called "Gospel." The Gospel of Mark and the Gospel of John are the other 2 gospel books. Scholars place the gospel of Matthew, Mark, and Luke in a category called "Synoptic Gospels."

The "Synoptic Gospels" have a great many similarities concerning the life, ministry, death, and resurrection of Jesus. They describe the same biblical events and stories about Jesus, though sometimes in different words, with more or fewer details.

Note of Interests: Biblical Scholars research revealed that approximately 97% of Mark's Gospel appears in Matthew and over 88% in Luke. Scholars believe that Mark's Gospel was the first gospel, and it was written between 50 and 70 AD. In the Gospel of John, approximately 90% of the information regarding Jesus' life is not in the other Gospels. John's Gospels contain many expressions and information about Jesus that is not in the Synoptic Gospels. Even though John's Gospel is unique, he presents a different side of Jesus that is complementary to the other 3 Gospels. His gospel provides an understanding of Jesus' divinity and pre-existence. John was the longest living disciple, and his Gospel was probably written last. John is also traditionally credited for writing 1st, 2nd, and 3rd John, as well as the Book of Revelation.

~~~~~~~~~~~~

Beginning in Matthew 9, verse 35, it's recorded that Jesus went to many towns and villages teaching in their synagogues, preaching the gospel of the kingdom of God. Jesus healed every kind of disease and sickness, among them. When Jesus saw the multitudes that followed him, he was moved with compassion for them. They were confused and helpless, like sheep without a shepherd.

According to Matthew 9:37, Jesus said to his disciples there is such a big harvest of people to bring in; but there are only a few workers to help them. Jesus told his disciples to pray that the Lord of the harvest would send forth laborers into his harvest.

In the 10th chapter of Matthew, Jesus called his 12 disciples together. He gave them power over evil spirits, power to heal the sick, and power over every kind of disease. After Jesus gave his disciples power, he now called the 12 disciples, Apostles. Listed below are the names of the first, 12 Apostles Jesus sent out:

1. Simon (also called Peter)
2. Andrew, the brother of Peter
3. James, the son of Zebedee
4. John, the brother of James
5. Philip
6. Bartholomew
7. Thomas
8. Matthew, the tax collector
9. James, the son of Alphaeus
10. Thaddaeus
11. Simon, the Zealot
12. Judas Iscariot, (the one who betrayed Jesus)

After Jesus called them forth, he gave them instructions, verses 5 – 15. The word "shoes" is embedded in these instructions, "Nor scrip for your journey, neither two coats, **neither shoes,** nor yet staves: for the workman is worthy of his meat," verse 10.

The 10th chapter of the Gospel of Matthew can be outlined as follow:

1. Jesus Chooses His Twelve Apostles, vs. 1 – 4
2. Instructions for the Twelve Apostles, vs. 5 – 15
3. Warning about Trouble, vs. 16 – 25
4. The One to Fear, vs. 26 – 31
5. Telling Others about Christ, vs. 32 – 33
6. Not Peace, but A Sword, vs. 34 – 39
7. Rewards, vs. 40 – 42

PS: I pray the title outline of the Gospel of Matthew 10 perks your curiosity, enough to make you take a moment and read the chapter in its entirety. *smile*

In the 10th chapter of Luke, Jesus appointed 72 others (disciples) and sent them out 2 by 2 ahead of him to every city, town, places where he would soon travel, Luke 10:1. The names of these 72 disciples are not giving in the Bible. Jesus instructed these 72 disciples to **carry neither money bag, knapsack, nor sandals;** and greet no one along the road. Whoever house they enter, Jesus instructed them to first say, "Peace to this house," Luke 10:4 – 5.

The 10th chapter of the Gospel of Luke can be outlined as follow:

1. Jesus Sends Out Seventy-Two more Disciples, vs. 1 – 12
2. The Unbelieving Cities, Towns, and Villages, vs. 13 – 16
3. The Return of the Seventy-Two Disciples, vs. 17 – 20
4. Jesus' Prayer of Thanks to His Father, vs. 21 – 24
5. Love the Lord with All Your Heart, Soul and Strength, and Mind, vs. 25 – 29
6. The Good Samaritan Parable, vs. 30 – 37
7. Jesus in the Home of Martha and Mary, vs. 38 – 41

In the 22nd chapter of Luke, Jesus asked the disciples a question at the Passover supper. Jesus asked the disciples, did they lacked anything when he sent them out among the people **without a purse, scrip, and shoes;** referring to Matthew 10:5 – 15. The disciples answered, no, to Jesus question, Luke 22:35.

According to Luke 22:36, Jesus told his disciples, "But now, if you have a purse, take it with you. He also told them to take a scrip, known as a traveling bag, and if you don't have a sword, sell some belongs to buy one." Luke 22 can be outlined as follows:

1. Judas, Part of the Plot to Kill Jesus, vs. 1 – 6
2. Jesus Eats with His Disciples, vs. 7 – 14
3. The Lord's Supper, vs. 14 – 23
4. An Argument about Greatness, vs. 24 – 30

5. Jesus Predicts Peter's Denial, vs. 31 – 34
6. Jesus tells his Disciples to take Moneybags, Traveling Bags, and Swords, vs. 35 – 38
7. Jesus Prays on Mount of Olives, vs. 39 – 46
8. Jesus is Betrayed by Judas and Arrested, vs. 47 – 53
9. Peter Says He Doesn't Know Jesus, vs. 54 – 65
10. Jesus is Questioned by the Council, vs. 66 – 71

Chapter 14

SHOES ON HIS FEET

Luke 15:22

But the father said to his servants, Bring forth the best robe, and put it on him; and put a ring on his hand, and **shoes on his feet.** KJV

But the father said to his servants, "Quick! Bring the best robe and put it on him. Put a ring on his finger and **sandals on his feet.** NIV

"But his father said to the servants, "Quick! Bring the finest robe in the house and put it on him. Get a ring for his fingers and **sandals for his feet.** NLT

~~~

The Gospel of Luke is the 3rd book in the New Testament, and it has 24 chapters. It was written by the Apostle Luke between 58 and 65 AD. Bible scholars believe the Gospel of Luke was written approximately 50 years after Jesus' death. The Book of Acts, also called "The Acts of the Apostles" was also written by the Apostle Luke addressed to Theophilus, Acts 1:1.

The Book of Acts recorded how the early Christian church under the leadership of Jesus' Apostles begins. The message of Jesus Christ begins in Jerusalem, spread to Judea and Samaria, then extended to the Roman Empire. The Book of Acts describes the activities, persecutions, trials, problems, and growth of the church during the middle of the 1st century.

The Gospel of Luke was written to the most excellent, Theophilus. Apostle Luke wrote it to him, so he could be sure of the truth of everything he was taught concerning the life and ministry of Jesus Christ, Luke 1:1 – 4.

That thou mightest know the certainty of those things, wherein thou hast been instructed.
Luke 1:4 KJV

Note of Interests: The Gospel of Luke and the Acts of the Apostles is addressed to an individual named "Theophilus." No one knows the true identity of Theophilus, but there are several opinions concerning his identity. Many scholars believe he was a Jew of Alexandria; others believe he was a converted Roman official. Traditions believe that Theophilus could have been Paul's lawyer during his trial period in Rome; others point to Theophilus ben Ananus, the High Priest for the Temple in Jerusalem. There are others who believe that "Theophilus" is an honorary title, not a person because "Theophilus" means "Friend of God." Therefore, both Luke and Acts would be addressed to anyone who fits that description.

~~~~~~~~~~~~

The Gospel of Luke can be outlined as follow:

Chapters 1 – 2	The Birth of John the Baptist and Jesus
Chapters 3 – 4:13	The Preparation of Jesus for His Public Ministry
Chapters 4:14 – 9:9	Jesus' Ministry in Galilee
Chapters 9:10 – 9:50	Jesus Travels to Regions around Galilee
Chapters 9:51 – 13:21	Jesus' Ministry in Judea
Chapters 13:22 – 19:27	Jesus' Ministry in and around Perea
Chapters 19:28 – 24:53	Jesus' Ministry Last Days

In the 15th chapter of Luke, it records 3 parables, Jesus spoke to the crowd.

1. The Lost Sheep, verses 1 – 7
2. The Lost Coin, verses 8 – 10
3. The Prodigal Son, verses 11 – 32

The words "shoes on his feet" is mentioned in the "Parable of the Prodigal Son," Luke 15:11 – 32. The father of the prodigal son had his servant to bring his returning son, the best robe, a ring for his finger, and shoes for his feet.

Jesus shares this parable with his disciples, the tax collectors, sinners, Pharisees and the teachers of the law. A man had 2 sons, whom he loved. The younger son told his father he wanted his share of the estate before he died. The father gave him his share.

Soon afterward, the younger son packed his belongings and went to a faraway foreign country. His extravagant living caused him to squander his fortune, eventually becoming destitute. He finally decided after working for a man to take care of pigs and being so hungry that he was willing to eat what the pigs were fed, to go back to his father. So, he left the foreign country going back to his father's house, hoping to be considered as a hired servant because he felt he was unworthy to be called his son.

According to Luke 15:20 – 24, while the prodigal son was a long way off, his father saw him coming. He ran to his son as fast as he could. He greets him with a hug and a kiss. His son told his father he had sinned against heaven and him. He stated, he no longer deserved to be called his son but make him a hired servant.

The father immediately told his servants to bring his son the best robe, a ring for his hand and shoes for his feet. The father then told the servant to cook the fattest calf so that they could celebrate his return. His son was dead in sin, but now he is alive again. He was lost among sinners, and now he is found.

The elder son had been in the field working, as he came near the house, he heard music and dancing. He asked one of the servants what was going on. The servant told him that is brother has returned home, and his father is having a celebration for him.

The elder son became angry and wouldn't go inside the house for the celebration. His father came outside and begged him to go inside. The elder son said to his father, "All these years I've served you, and always obeyed what you said, and never once have I refused to do a single thing you told me to. But in all that time you never gave me one young goat for a feast with my friends; but when this son of yours comes back after squandering his money on harlots, you celebrate his return by killing the fattest calf!"

According to the last two verses of this chapter, the father spoke to his elder son. He said to him, "Look, dear son, you have always stayed by me, and everything I have is yours. It is right and good that we should have a celebration and be happy this day. For your brother was dead and is alive again; he was lost, but now he is found!" Luke 15:31 – 32.

A Reader's Question

This new section just dropped in my spirit at 0613 on January 14, 2017, titled A Reader's Question.

An individual asked me the following question: "Whose resource information on the subjects I write about, do I trust the most?"

The Answer:

I have no particular resource I trust the most.

There are many different beliefs, interpretations, and explanations among Scholars, church denominations, and people.

I try to grasp the main concept, and not be too critical.

Then, I pray, fast, and seek Father's guidance on what to write for each subject title.

**In all thy ways acknowledge him,
and He shall direct thy paths.**
Proverbs 3:6

Author's Closing Remarks

It never ceases to amaze me how the LORD often arouses my interest in a subject and then He drives me to his Word to explore the Biblical truths and events for His godly inspiration.

This book about shoes certainly enlightened and entertained me. I hope and pray it did the same for you. I hope it was not just interesting but motivate you to be a better Christian. Praise God! I just couldn't resist . . . *smile*

Jot down a word or two that come to your mind on the following shoe titles:

Put Off Thy Shoes _____

Shoes on Your Feet _____

Thy Shoes _____

Old Shoes _____

In His Shoes _____

Feet with Shoes _____

Shoes be Broken _____

Shoes Upon Thy Feet _____

For a Pair of Shoes _____

Whose Shoes _____

Neither, Nor, Without Shoes _____

Shoes on His Feet _____

Now, how many chapters do you have to re-read? Oh Yes, re-read . . . _____
Just pray and smile . . Be blessed in Jesus' Name

Pray for the Ministry . . . May the "LORD of Peace," give you His Peace.

Dr. Vanessa

References

Chapter 1
1. Wikipedia, The Free Encyclopedia: https://en.wikipedia.org/wiki/Shoe
2. BibleGateway: https://www.biblegateway.com

Chapter 2
1. BibleGateway: https://www.biblegateway.com
2. Jacksonville Theology Seminary

Chapter 3
1. BibleGateway: https://www.biblegateway.com
2. Isaiah 26:3 – 4 "Perfect Peace" The Last Single Digit

Chapter 4
1. Wikipedia, The Free Encyclopedia: https://en.wikipedia.org/wiki/Passover
2. BibleGateway: https://www.biblegateway.com

Chapter 5
1. Jacksonville Theology Seminary
2. BibleGateway: https://www.biblegateway.com

Chapter 6
1. BibleGateway: https://www.biblegateway.com
2. Wikipedia, The Free Encyclopedia: https://en.wikipedia.org/wiki/Gibeon_(ancient_city)

Chapter 7
1. BibleGateway: https://www.biblegateway.com

Chapter 8
1. Wikipedia, The Free Encyclopedia: https://en.wikipedia.org/wiki/Songs_of_Songs
2. Wikipedia, The Free Encyclopedia: https://en.wikipedia.org/wiki/Mandrake

Chapter 9
1. BibleGateway: https://www.biblegateway.com
2. Wikipedia, The Free Encyclopedia: https://en.wikipedia.org/wiki/Isaiah

Chapter 10
1. Wikipedia, The Free Encyclopedia: https://en.wikipedia.org/wiki/Book_of_Ezekiel
2. BibleGateway: https://www.biblegateway.com
3. Jacksonville Theology Seminary

Chapter 11
1. BibleGateway: https://www.biblegateway.com
2. Jacksonville Theology Seminary

Chapter 12
1. BibleGateway: https://www.biblegateway.com
2. Wikipedia, The Free Encyclopedia: https://en.wikipedia.org/wiki/Gospel
3. Jacksonville Theology Seminary

Chapter 13
1. BibleGateway: https://www.biblegateway.com

Chapter 14

1. BibleGateway: https://www.biblegateway.com
2. Jacksonville Theology Seminary
3. Wikipedia, The Free Encyclopedia: https://en.wikipedia.org/wiki/Theophilus_(biblical)

Answers & Information Section

Chapter 2   Biblical Sandals
According to Genesis 3:7, "And the eyes of them (Adam and Eve) were opened, and they knew they were naked; and they sewed **fig leaves** together and made themselves aprons."

Chapter 4   Shoes on Your Feet   Exodus 12:11
The 10 plagues are listed below:

1.	Water Turned into Blood	Exodus 7:14-25
2.	Frogs	Exodus 8:1-15
3.	Lice	Exodus 8:16-19
4.	Flies	Exodus 8:20-32
5.	Diseased Livestock	Exodus 9:1-7
6.	Boils	Exodus 9:8-12
7.	Hail	Exodus 9:13-35
8.	Locusts	Exodus 10:1-20
9.	Darkness for 3 Days	Exodus 10:21-29
10.	Death of the Firstborn	Exodus 12:29 -32

Chapter 9   Shoes be Broken   Isaiah 5:27
The names of the 4 kings in the southern kingdom of Judah.

1. Uzziah
2. Jotham
3. Ahaz
4. Hezekiah

Other Books by the Author:

From the Pew to the Pulpit	Published: 08/29/2007
Isaiah 26:3-4 "Perfect Peace"	Published: 09/07/2010
Isaiah 26:3-4 "Perfect Peace" The Last Single Digit	Published: 02/13/2012
Isaiah 26:3-4 "Perfect Peace III" Silver and Gold	Published: 10/24/2012
Isaiah 26:3-4 "Perfect Peace IV" The Kingdom Number	Published: 04/10/2013
Isaiah 26:3-4 "Perfect Peace V" 2541	Published: 09/06/2013
Isaiah 26:3-4 "Perfect Peace VI" Zacchaeus	Published: 02/28/2014
Isaiah 26:3-4 "Perfect Peace VII" Eleven	Published: 10/29/2014
Isaiah 26:3-4 "Perfect Peace VIII" Prayer	Published: 05/22/2015
Isaiah 26:3-4 "Perfect Peace IX" Sixteen	Published: 10/26/2015
Isaiah 26:3-4 "Perfect Peace X" Dreams	Published: 04/12/2016
Isaiah 26:3-4 "Perfect Peace XI" Door	Published: 02/13/2017
Isaiah 26:3-4 "Perfect Peace XII" River	Published: 08/02/2017
Isaiah 26:3-4 "Perfect Peace XIII" 1 Kings 19:1-18	Published: 12/18/2017

Printed in the United States
By Bookmasters